W9-ASN-992

Searchlight
BOOKS™

Climate Change

Climate Change and Life on Earth

Chinwe Onuoha

Lerner Publications ◆ Minneapolis

To every student who reads this book

Lerner Publications Company
A division of Lerner Publishing Group, Inc.
241 First Avenue North
Minneapolis, MN 55401 USA

For reading levels and more information, look up this title
at www.lernerbooks.com.

Main body text set in Adrianna Regular 14/20.
Typeface provided by Chank.

Library of Congress Cataloging-in-Publication Data

Names: Onuoha, Chinwe, 1991- author.
Title: Climate change and life on Earth / Chinwe Onuoha.
Description: Minneapolis : Lerner Publications, [2019] | Series: Searchlight
    books. Climate change | Audience: Ages 8-11. | Audience: Grades 4 to 6. |
    Includes bibliographical references and index.
Identifiers: LCCN 2018016823 (print) | LCCN 2018027517 (ebook) | ISBN
    9781541543676 (eb pdf) | ISBN 9781541538672 (lb : alk. paper) | ISBN
    9781541545922 (pb : alk. paper)
Subjects: LCSH: Climatic changes—Juvenile literature. | Climatic
    changes—Effect of human beings on—Juvenile literature. | Human
    ecology—Juvenile literature.
Classification: LCC QC903.15 (ebook) | LCC QC903.15 .O58 2019 (print) | DDC
    551.6—dc23
LC record available at https://lccn.loc.gov/2018016823

Manufactured in the United States of America
1-45050-35877-6/12/2018

Contents

Chapter 1

WHAT IS CLIMATE CHANGE?

Let's face it: Earth's climate is changing. Temperatures are rising, polar ice is melting, and weather-related storms are getting stronger. Changes like these are happening worldwide and affecting all living creatures on Earth.

Hurricane Harvey hit Texas in August 2017. It had the most rainfall for any tropical storm ever recorded.

Meteorologists use computers to track patterns in temperatures, rainfall, and wind to predict weather.

Climate vs. Weather

Climate is different from weather. Weather is what happens in a place's atmosphere. Rain, snow, and wind are all examples of weather. Weather changes every day. Climate is a place's average weather conditions over time. For example, Florida's climate is warm and sunny because the weather there is usually warm and sunny.

But what if Florida's average temperature dropped so much that it started snowing regularly? That would be an example of climate change. Climate change is a change in Earth's weather patterns over a long time.

It's Getting Hot in Here

Temperatures are rising around the world. But why? It has to do with greenhouse gases. These are certain kinds of gases that trap some of the sun's heat in Earth's atmosphere. Without greenhouse gases, all the sun's heat would escape back into space at night. Then Earth would be too cold for plants and animals to live. But too much greenhouse gas in the atmosphere causes Earth to get too hot.

Carbon dioxide is the most common greenhouse gas. Exhaust from cars and power plants puts carbon dioxide in our atmosphere.

Methane is another greenhouse gas. It leaks into the air during extraction of natural gas from the ground.

More greenhouse gases are in the atmosphere than ever before. But how are they getting there? Humans are to blame. People use fossil fuels such as coal, oil, and natural gas for energy to heat their homes and drive their cars. When fossil fuels burn, they release greenhouse gases. This increases Earth's temperatures and leads to climate change.

Chapter 2

CLIMATE CHANGE AFFECTS LIFE ON LAND

Climate change affects our planet in many ways. As Earth gets warmer, it also gets drier. Glaciers start to melt. These changes threaten all plants and animals.

The golden toad is extinct. Climate change destroyed its habitat.

Drought limits our food supply because it damages farmers' crops. Crops such as corn can't survive without rain.

Drought

Climate change can cause drought, which is a long period of dryness. Weather during a drought is usually dry and hot. Drought occurs when a place gets very little rainfall or snow for a long time.

Droughts can devastate farms. When rainfall decreases, it's harder for farmers to water their plants and produce crops. But droughts are dangerous for animals and other plants too.

Dry Spell

Low quantities of water make it difficult for most plants to survive. Without water, plants can't produce as much food. They also overheat more quickly, so they may dry out and die. All kinds of plants—from trees to flowers to grass—suffer in a drought.

If soil gets too dry, it turns to dust. As winds pick it up, dust storms can occur.

▲

IF THEY CAN'T FIND FOOD OR WATER IN THEIR OWN HABITAT, WILD ANIMALS MIGHT LOOK FOR IT IN CITIES.

As plants die, animals that rely on them for food suffer too. For farmers who raise cows or chickens, dying grass in fields means not enough for the animals to eat. And too little water makes it difficult to keep the livestock hydrated. In severe cases of drought, animals may get sick and even die.

Burning Up

One of the greatest threats to the lives of plants and animals is wildfires. If a wildfire starts in a climate with enough moisture, it burns slowly. Firefighters are usually able to reach the fire quickly and put it out before it causes too much damage.

But if a wildfire starts on land suffering from drought, the fire spreads quickly. These wildfires are very difficult to put out. They can burn for days. Wildfires like this kill everything in their path.

The Thomas Fire of 2017 was the largest wildfire in California. It burned for over a month and destroyed more than one thousand buildings.

Just like rivers, glaciers move! Antarctica's Lambert Glacier is the largest glacier in the world. It moves about 1,310 to 2,620 feet (400 m to 800 m) per year.

Melting Ice

Climate change is also affecting Earth's glaciers. Glaciers are large masses of ice made up of layers of snow. Glaciers are on every continent except Australia. They cover 10 percent of Earth's land.

As temperatures increase, glaciers are melting very fast. For example, Alaska's Glacier National Park has lost more than 120 of its 150 glaciers since 1910.

The glaciers in the mountains of central Asia are melting too. As they melt and temperatures rise, people are planting crops and raising livestock higher up on the mountainsides. This migration is shrinking the habitat of the endangered snow leopards near the mountaintops.

As the habitat of snow leopards gets smaller, their food supply decreases. This forces many snow leopards to come down the mountainside and kill people's livestock for food. As the glaciers continue to melt, snow leopards will be at even greater risk of extinction.

Snow leopards are in danger of extinction. Scientists believe that only about six thousand snow leopards live in the wild.

Chapter 3

CLIMATE CHANGE AFFECTS OCEAN LIFE

Climate change also affects plants and animals that live in the ocean. Melting glaciers, melting sea ice, and more acidic ocean waters are three of the ways climate change threatens ocean life.

Due to climate change, global sea levels have risen by 8 inches (20 cm) over the last century. This also affects ocean life.

Rivers of Dirt

When a glacier melts, its runoff carries sediment, or sand and clay, into rivers, lakes, and oceans. In the waters surrounding Antarctica, this sediment affects many tiny filter feeders. They filter through the water to find food. If ocean water is too dirty, filter feeders won't get enough to eat. When they die, larger animals that eat filter feeders, such as sharks, will go hungry too.

In Antarctic waters, the diverse ecosystem attracts krill, which whales eat. Melting glaciers could limit the food supply of these whales.

The amount of light a surface reflects is its albedo. Sea ice has a high albedo. It reflects a lot of light.

On Thin Ice

Sea ice is different from glaciers. Glaciers form on land and are made of packed snow. Sea ice is frozen ocean water. It forms in the cold winter months and melts in warm summer months. Sea ice is in the polar regions of the Arctic and Antarctic Oceans.

Sea ice is white, so it reflects a lot of light from the sun. It doesn't absorb much of the sun's heat, and it helps keep the polar regions cold.

Since 1980, ocean animals have lost about seven weeks of sea ice.

As Earth's temperatures increase, sea ice freezes later in the winter each year and melts earlier in the spring. But many ocean animals need sea ice to survive.

Ice algae live under sea ice. These plants use tiny amounts of light to make food. Ice algae feeds many ocean creatures, such as tiny floating animals called zooplankton. Larger fish eat zooplankton, and then birds, seals, and whales eat them. As sea ice melts, the habitat of ice algae disappears. Without ice algae, the whole Arctic food chain could starve.

Melting sea ice affects larger species of animals too. Endangered polar bears walk on sea ice to hunt for food. Without it, polar bears are stuck in one area and have to compete with other animals for food.

Walruses also need sea ice. They hunt for clams and small ocean creatures in shallow water, and they rest on sea ice. As sea ice melts, large groups of walruses are forced to hunt in the same areas on land.

A GATHERING OF WALRUSES ON LAND IS CALLED A HAULOUT.

▼

The ocean isn't the only water becoming acidic. When air pollutants mix with water in the atmosphere, it creates acid rain. Acid rain destroys Earth's plants.

Changing Ocean Water

Oceans are excellent at storing heat. The top several feet of water holds just as much heat as Earth's atmosphere. Some heat is good. If oceans are too cold, many plants and animals will die. But as the temperature of Earth's atmosphere increases, the oceans get warmer too. Warmer water could be deadly for ocean life such as salmon, penguins, and bowhead whales.

STEM In Depth: All-Female Sea Turtles

As the temperature of ocean water increases, the sand surrounding the water also gets warmer. The temperature of sand affects the sex of sea turtle hatchlings. In fact, 99 percent of turtle hatchlings in northern Australia, where waters are warmer than southern Australia, are female. As temperatures increase worldwide, even fewer male sea turtles will hatch. Without males to aid in reproduction, sea turtles would face extinction.

If the temperature of the sand surrounding green sea turtle eggs gets higher than 84.7°F (29.3°C), only female turtles will hatch.

Brittle stars are very sensitive to acidic oceans. If water is too acidic, they cannot generate new limbs and their larvae die before becoming adults.

Acidic Oceans

The ocean also stores a lot of carbon dioxide. It absorbs about 25 percent of all the carbon dioxide that humans release into the atmosphere. However, higher levels of carbon dioxide make the ocean more acidic.

Acidic water contains more acid, which affects all kinds of ocean life. While many adult fish can adapt to more acidic waters, their eggs have trouble developing. For example, baby clown fish that hatch in acidic waters don't smell as well as other clown fish. This stops them from sensing danger, so many die before they are able to reproduce.

Dissolving Shells

More carbon dioxide in ocean waters also reduces the amount of calcium carbonate there. Many ocean creatures create their protective shells from it. Oysters and clams cannot live in acidic oceans because the acid dissolves their shells. Without shells, they cannot live. And without these shellfish, larger predators that eat them will starve.

ACIDIC OCEAN WATER IS KILLING CORAL. MANY OTHER ANIMALS USE CORAL FOR FOOD AND SHELTER.

Forests also absorb carbon dioxide from the atmosphere. Trees take in carbon dioxide, which is made of carbon and oxygen, and convert it to food. The trees release oxygen back into the air and store the carbon in their trunks. Scientists call forests carbon sinks. They absorb more carbon dioxide than they release.

But some forests are becoming carbon sources. They release more carbon dioxide than they absorb. Trees that are cut down or that die from drought or wildfires release carbon dioxide.

About fifteen billion trees are cut down each year. When we cut down trees for wood or to clear space, even more carbon dioxide is released into the atmosphere.

Chapter 4

SAVING LIFE ON EARTH

Climate change is a global issue. People worldwide are finding ways to protect Earth's plants and animals. Wildlife groups in Australia, for instance, are working to save the albatross. Heavy rainfall and higher temperatures are destroying this bird's nests. Not having nests makes it hard for chicks to survive. Scientists are building concrete nests and placing them in trees. So more albatross chicks are surviving.

An albatross lays only one egg at a time. If the egg dies, the albatross will not lay another one until the following year.

Laws can help plants and animals too. In 1973, President Richard Nixon signed the Endangered Species Act. It is considered the United States' strongest conservation law, and it's still in effect today. This act encourages Americans to protect plants and animals facing extinction. As of 2016, the act protects more than twenty-two hundred species.

The Endangered Species Act has saved more than 230 plant and animal species from extinction, including the bald eagle.

Scientists have even learned that boosting animal populations helps fight climate change. Sea otters are a good example. In the early twentieth century, they were almost extinct. But as soon as the sea otter population started improving, something unexpected happened. Seagrass and other ocean plants multiplied! Scientists have calculated that the ocean plants in the otters' regions have absorbed more than 8 million tons (7.3 million t) of carbon dioxide per year!

If people work to reduce climate change, life should improve for Earth's plants and animals.

The wildebeests of Africa shape their ecosystem. When their population is healthy, the grasses of their habitat grow better and absorb more carbon dioxide.

What You Can Do

We can do so much to protect Earth's plants and animals!
Here are some ways you can help:

- **Use less water by taking shorter showers.** Conserving water will reduce the effects of drought.

- **Plant a garden or a tree.** This will reduce carbon dioxide in the air and support the health of wildlife.

- **Take a walk, ride a bike, or ride the bus instead of riding in a car.** Then you won't increase greenhouse gases in the atmosphere.

- **Buy your foods from local markets.** Using trucks to transport food long distances increases greenhouse gases.

Climate Change Timeline

1970   The US National Oceanic and Atmospheric Administration is formed to research and predict changes in Earth's climate.

1973   President Richard Nixon signs the Endangered Species Act.

1988   The United Nations starts the Intergovernmental Panel on Climate Change to analyze climate data.

2008   Polar bears and beluga whales are added to the Endangered Species list.

2015   The Paris Agreement to fight climate change and reduce the amount of greenhouse gas put into the air is adopted by 195 nations.

Glossary

acidic: something that contains acid, or has a pH below 7. Acidic liquids, such as vinegar, taste sour.

atmosphere: a layer of gases that surrounds a planet

calcium carbonate: a solid substance found in bones and shells

climate: the average weather conditions of a region over a long time

climate change: changes in average weather conditions

conservation: preservation and protection of something

drought: a long period of dry weather

food chain: an order of organisms or animals in which each uses the one beneath it as a food source

fossil fuel: a source of energy, such as coal, oil, or natural gas, formed from the buildup of dead plants and animals

greenhouse gas: gas that traps heat from the sun in the atmosphere. Carbon dioxide and methane are greenhouse gases.

habitat: the place or environment where a plant or animal naturally lives

weather: conditions in the air above Earth, such as wind, rain, or temperature

Learn More about Life on Earth

Books

Castaldo, Nancy F. *Mission: Polar Bear Rescue: All about Polar Bears and How to Save Them*. Washington, DC: National Geographic Society, 2014. Get up close with polar bears, and learn how to protect them from climate change.

Meister, Cari. *Droughts*. Minneapolis: Pogo Books, 2016. Learn how to prevent the devastating effects of drought.

Newman, Patricia. *Sea Otter Heroes: The Predators That Saved an Ecosystem*. Minneapolis: Millbrook Press, 2017. Discover how protecting animals can affect a whole ecosystem.

Websites

Kids against Climate Change
https://kidsagainstclimatechange.co/start-learning/
Explore the effects of climate change through videos, games, activities, and more.

NASA Climate Kids: Plants and Animals
https://climatekids.nasa.gov/menu/plants-and-animals/
Discover all the ways that climate change is affecting Earth's plants and animals.

National Geographic Kids: What Is Climate Change?
https://www.natgeokids.com/au/discover/geography/general
-geography/what-is-climate-change/#!/register
Find out more about how climate change happens and can be prevented.

Index

Photo Acknowledgments

Image credits: Marcus Yam/Los Angeles Times/Getty Images, p. 4; Matthew Peyton/Getty Images, p. 5; 1968/Shutterstock.com, p. 6; robertwcoy/Shutterstock.com, p. 7; Michael & Patricia Fogden/ Minden Pictures/Getty Images, p. 8; CraneStation/Flickr (CC BY 2.0), p. 9; Franklin D. Roosevelt Presidential Library, p. 10; Robert McGuoey/All Canada Photo/Getty Images, p. 11; © Kari Greer/ US Forest Service (CC BY 2.0), p. 12; Colin Monteath/Hedgehog House/Minden Pictures/Newscom, p. 13; Don Johnston/All Canada Photos/Getty Images, p. 14; Eko Siswono Toyudho/Anadolu Agency/ Getty Images, p. 15; Doug Allan/The Image Bank/Getty Images, p. 16; John B. Weller photo, courtesy of The Pew Charitable Trusts, United State Department of State, p. 17; FloridaStock/ Shutterstock.com, p. 18; Jeff Foott/Discovery Channel Images/Getty Images, p. 19; Richard Packwood/Oxford Scientific/Getty Images, p. 20; kjorgen/iStock/Getty Images, p. 21; Linda Pitkin/ Nature Picture Library/Getty Images, p. 22; Borisoff/Shutterstock.com, p. 23; svic/Shutterstock. com, p. 24; Otto Plantema/Buiten-beeld/Minden Pictures/Getty Images, p. 25; Elizabeth W. Kearley/Moment/Getty Images, p. 26; Godong/Universal Images Group/Getty Images, p. 27.

Cover: Georgette Douwma/Photographer's Choice/Getty Images.